GRAND SLAM TRIVIA

GRAND SLAM TRIVIA

Secrets, statistics, and little-known facts about pro baseball

Bruce Adelson

illustrations by
Harry Pulver Jr.

Lerner Publications Company, Minneapolis

For Sharon Craig, Vicki Fagliorone, Laurie Goss, Sally Keyes, Jan McConnel, and Lorraine Nasiatka—second grade teachers at Zachary Taylor Elementary School in Arlington, Virginia. Your dedication, collegiality, and professionalism will inspire me for years to come. Thank you.

—B.A.

The assistance of Blythe Apple, Katie Kramer, Chris McCartin, and Carl Siegmund of Joan Yocum's fifth grade language arts class at Zachary Taylor Elementary School is gratefully acknowledged. Your exuberance and helpful review of this book contributed to its completion. Thanks as well to Joan Yocum, whose enthusiasm for our writing project will always be appreciated.

—B.A.

Library of Congress Cataloging-in-Publication Data

Adelson, Bruce.
    Grand slam trivia / by Bruce Adelson ; illustrations by Harry Pulver Jr.
      p. cm. — (Sports trivia)
    Includes bibliographical references and index.
    Summary: Presents an assortment of anecdotes and information about the history, rules, equipment, and personalities of the game of baseball.
    ISBN 0–8225–3314–6 (lib. bdg. : alk. paper)
    ISBN 0–8225–9803–5 (pbk. : alk. paper)
    1. Baseball—Miscellanea—Juvenile literature. [1. Baseball—Miscellanea.]
    I. Pulver, Harry, ill. II. Title. III. Series.
    GV867.5.A34 1998
    796.357—dc21   97–42297

Illustrations by Harry Pulver Jr.
Book design and electronic prepress: Steve Foley, Mike Kohn, Sean Todd

This book is available in two editions:
Library binding by Lerner Publications Company
Soft cover by First Avenue Editions
241 First Avenue North, Minneapolis, Minnesota 55401

Lerner

Manufactured in the United States of America
1 2 3 4 5 6 – JR – 04 03 02 01 00 99

Contents

Chapter 1

The Game of Baseball

Did You Know?

Baseball in some form has been played in North America for more than 200 years. There is evidence that a type of baseball was even played by George Washington's soldiers at Valley Forge during the American Revolutionary War.

Baseball began as a combination of several other games, including the English sport of cricket. In the 1830s and 1840s, a distinctive game of baseball began to develop in Canada and the United States. Many people believe that the first modern baseball game was played in Ontario, Canada, on June 4, 1838. That game was the first reported to have used a home plate and fair and foul territory on the field. Runs back then were called tallies. Tallies were recorded by cutting notches in a stick each time a runner scored.

Seven years after the game in Ontario, Alexander Cartwright and his team—the Knickerbockers—played a baseball game in New York City. Cartwright, often considered the Father of Baseball, developed a system of rules, many of which are still in use. Cartwright's game used a diamond-shaped field. He is credited with developing the "three-strikes-and-you're-out" rule. Cartwright also established the standard of three outs per side and originated the nine-person team. For the rest of the nineteenth century, the sport of baseball became increasingly more popular. The game was even played by soldiers during the Civil War.

Alexander Cartwright

Did You Know?

In 1869 the first professional baseball team, the Cincinnati Red Stockings, began to play. Since 1959 this team has been known as the Cincinnati Reds.

In the early days of baseball, players did not use gloves. They were expected to use their bare hands to catch the hard ball. Players back then were accustomed to how a hard ball felt. In baseball's early days, you could also get someone out by hitting a baserunner with a thrown baseball.

The first gloves were used in the 1870s, but they were different from modern gloves. The early gloves were very thin, with no padding or webbing. They were designed only to provide slight protection for a fielder's hands. Modern gloves have pockets to help fielders catch the ball, and they have padding—thicker than in old-fashioned gloves—to protect the players' hands.

Did You Know?

In 1894 Jerry Denny retired after playing professional baseball for 13 years. He was the last professional baseball player to not use a glove.

Who are the only two fielders on a baseball diamond who don't wear gloves?

Turn to page 56 for the answer.

The Abner Doubleday baseball sits on display at the National Baseball Museum. In the early 1900s, some baseball fans—including sporting-goods manufacturer Albert Spalding—credited Doubleday with the invention of the game.

Baseball bats and balls have also changed since the early days of the game, but not as much as gloves have. Balls are rounder than they used to be. In the early days, baseballs were made from twisted yarn covered by calfskin. Modern balls are painted white, with bright red stitching, so they are easy for hitters and fielders to see.

Major league baseball bats have always been made of wood. Bats used by high school and college teams are made of aluminum. Aluminum bats are generally lighter and easier to swing than wooden ones, and they can't break. Softball players also use aluminum bats.

Modern wood bats are rounder and more uniform than early bats. Bats used in major league baseball cannot be more than 42 inches long. In early baseball, there was no limit to the length of the bats.

If you look carefully at a major league bat that has been used in a game, you will see that the middle of the bat and the bat handle are usually darker than the other parts. That is because these parts of the bat are covered with a material called pine tar. Pine tar is dark and sticky. It is made from a substance that is found in pine trees. Batters rub pine tar on their bats or their hands to get a better grip on the bat handle.

Wooden bats, some smeared with pine tar, stand in a line outside the dugout.

Q: *What will you find if you cut open a baseball?*

A: *The inside of a modern baseball is made of cork and rubber and yarn, covered by two strips of white horsehide or cowhide.* The cork inside the baseball helps it travel farther than its ancestors did.

Did You Know?

All baseball players wear a pair of socks called stirrups. The stirrups match the colors of the player's team. Players either pull their uniform pants over the stirrups or wear the stirrups on top of their pants. Underneath the stirrups, all players today wear a pair of white socks that are called sanitary hose.

Baseball players did not always wear white socks underneath their colored ones. Here is the story of how this practice began. In 1905, a player named Napoleon Lajoie (LASH-uh-way) had his foot cut by another player sliding into him while he played second base. In the early days of baseball, players wore long, thick, wool stockings. Lajoie's wool stockings were dyed blue. The blue dye from the stockings leaked into his cut and gave Lajoie a bad case of blood poisoning.

It is thought that after Lajoie's injury, players were required to wear white undersocks to protect them from injury and blood poisoning. Since the white socks were supposed to be "sanitary," or clean and white, to protect players from harm, they became known as sanitary hose.

But what ever happened to Napoleon Lajoie? He recovered from his case of blood poisoning and went on to a great career in baseball, playing for 21 years and batting .338. In 1901, Napoleon Lajoie batted .422, the sixth highest season batting average in baseball history. In 1937 he became a member of the Baseball Hall of Fame.

Napoleon Lajoie sports his wool stockings.

Did You Know?

The New York Yankees in 1929 were the first base-ball team to put numbers on the backs of their uniforms. The numbers helped fans tell who the players were and where they batted in the lineup. If you batted second, your uniform number was 2. Babe Ruth batted third so his number was 3. Lou Gehrig was number 4 because he batted fourth in the lineup.

Lou Gehrig (left) and Babe Ruth (right) share a joke. The two baseball legends played together for the New York Yankees— Gehrig for 17 years; Ruth for 15 years.

Trivia Teaser #2

Did bulls ever live in a baseball bullpen? Where did the word bullpen come from?

Professional baseball's longest game took place in Rhode Island on April 18, 1981, between two teams in the minor leagues, the Pawtucket (Rhode Island) Red Sox and Rochester (New York) Red Wings. That game, scheduled to start at 7 P.M., was delayed for more than 30 minutes because of an electric power failure. When the game finally began,

the temperature was around 30 degrees, and a cold, strong wind was blowing into Pawtucket's stadium from over the centerfield fence.

After 32 innings, 8 hours and 25 minutes, the umpires stopped the game with the score tied 2–2. At that time, the temperature was 10 degrees above zero, and only about 20 fans were still in the ballpark. When the game was restarted two months later, Pawtucket quickly scored one run in the 33rd inning, finally ending baseball's longest game. Wade Boggs and Cal Ripken Jr. are two famous players who played in baseball's longest game.

Mike Hart, who later played in the major leagues with the Texas Rangers, will never forget the game in Pawtucket. "The wind was blowing in so hard you couldn't hit anything. There were guys in the clubhouse who had gone to sleep and woke back up when they had to play in the game. I felt so sleepy I could barely keep my eyes open. The pitcher looked like he threw 150 miles per hour. I didn't have a chance. He struck me out."

Trivia Teaser #3

How many innings are there in a normal baseball game?

Chapter 2

Feats in the Negro Leagues and in the Major Leagues

In 1884, Moses "Fleet" Walker became the first African American to play major league baseball. But for the next 62 years, no other African Americans were allowed to play in the majors. They were kept out of the big leagues for only one reason, because of their skin color.

The first black league—the Negro National League—was founded in 1920. Through the 1920s and 1930s, teams and leagues often dissolved, rearranged, and reappeared. In the late 1930s, two regional leagues—the Negro National League and the Negro American League—played out regular seasons. The winning team from each league met for a black world series each fall.

Major League Baseball's policy of discrimination, known as the "color line," ended in 1947, when one black ballplayer crossed the line to play in the big leagues. From then on, the Negro leagues lost more and more of their best black players to the major leagues, and by 1949, the Negro leagues had faded out of the picture.

Q: Who became the first African American to play major league baseball in the twentieth century?

A. Larry Doby

B. Willie Mays

C. Jackie Robinson

D. Hank Aaron

Turn the page for the answer.

C. Jackie Robinson. In 1947, 28-year-old Robinson began playing major league baseball. He was under tremendous pressure because no other African American had played in the major leagues for more than 60 years. Many people believed blacks and whites should not play baseball together and taunted Robinson. He received hate mail. People threatened that if Robinson continued to play in the major leagues, he and his wife would be shot and his son kidnapped. Some players on other major league teams also made things difficult for Robinson, yelling things at him and pointing their bats like guns in his direction while making shooting noises.

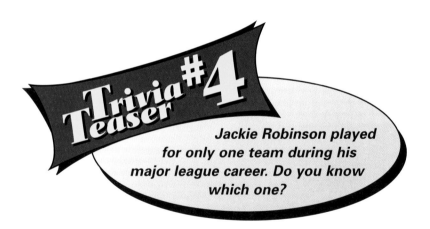

Trivia Teaser #4

Jackie Robinson played for only one team during his major league career. Do you know which one?

Everyone knew that if Jackie Robinson played badly, it would be more difficult for other African Americans to follow him and play in the majors since many people thought that black players were not talented enough to handle big league baseball. If Robinson could not do it, they might say, why should other African Americans be given a chance?

Jackie Robinson signs autographs for young fans in 1947.

Although Robinson struggled in his first season, he eventually became comfortable and had an excellent year. He batted .297 and was named the 1947 National League Rookie of the Year. Jackie Robinson played major league baseball for 10 seasons, batting .311 for his career. He was elected to the Baseball Hall of Fame in 1962.

Q: *Eight members of the Baseball Hall of Fame played in both the Negro leagues and the major leagues. Can you name them?*

A: **Hank Aaron, Ernie Banks, Roy Campanella, Monte Irvin, Willie Mays, Satchel Paige, Billy Williams and Jackie Robinson.** Jackie played shortstop for the Kansas City Monarchs in 1945. He was one of the best players in the league that season, batting .345. The Negro leagues have a strong connection to modern baseball. For example, Lyle Mouton of the Chicago White Sox had two relatives, Wallace and Stanley, who played in the Negro leagues. Wallace, Lyle's grandfather, even played against Jackie Robinson.

Cool Papa Bell slides into third base. Bell was one of the top base stealers in baseball history.

Did You Know?

James Thomas Bell played professional baseball for 28 years, beginning in 1922. Considered one of the best ballplayers in history and the fastest player ever, Bell stole 175 bases in 200 games during the 1933 season. In 1920, he won a race against Jimmy Lyons, thought to be the fastest man in the Negro leagues. As a reward, Bell was given a brand new pair of the best baseball spikes.

Nicknamed Cool Papa, Bell was once clocked circling the bases on the baseball field in only 12 seconds, which is thought to be the fastest anyone has ever run the bases. Bell, who once stole two bases on a single pitch, was so quick that pitcher Satchel Paige remarked, "Bell was so fast, he could flip off the light and get into bed before the room got dark." Cool Papa Bell never played in the major leagues, finishing his career in 1950. He was elected into the Baseball Hall of Fame in 1974.

Trivia Teaser #5

Although Cool Papa Bell may have been the fastest player ever, which player holds the major league baseball record for most stolen bases in a single season?

Did You Know?

Josh Gibson was the greatest home run hitter in Negro leagues history. It is believed that he hit 962 home runs in his 17-year career, from 1930 to 1946. In 1931 Gibson hit 75 home runs, thought to be the most home runs ever hit by a profession-al baseball player in one season in North America. In his career, he played for only two teams, the Homestead Grays and Pittsburgh Crawfords. Josh Gibson never played in the major leagues. He was elected to Base-ball's Hall of Fame in 1972.

Josh Gibson

Who holds the major league record for hitting the most career home runs?

A. Babe Ruth
B. Willie Mays
C. Hank Aaron
D. Mickey Mantle

Trivia Teaser #6

"I played Little League but I stopped playing baseball until my junior year of high school. I wasn't really into baseball. Basically, I played basketball and football through high school. But people said I was a decent baseball player, so I kept playing." I play for the New York Yankees, and I have hit more home runs in the 1990s than any other baseball player. My nickname is Big Daddy because I hit a lot of home runs and I am a big guy. Babe Ruth and I have done something no other players have.
WHO AM I?

C. Hank Aaron. Aaron holds the record with 755 home runs in his 22-year major league career.

Hank Aaron began his big league career in 1954 with the Milwaukee Braves. The Braves had moved to Milwaukee, Wisconsin, from Boston, Massachusetts, in 1952. In 1966, the Braves moved again, finding a new home in Atlanta, Georgia, which remains the Braves' hometown.

When Aaron ended his career in 1976, he was playing for his second Milwaukee team. This team, known as the Brewers, still plays in Wisconsin. The Brewers had moved to Milwaukee from Seattle, Washington, in 1970. Over the years, many teams like the Braves and the Brewers have moved around from city to city.

Hank Aaron cracks another home run. Aaron also holds the major league record for runs batted in (RBIs), with 2,297.

Q: *Which player held the major league home run record before Hank Aaron broke it in 1974?*

A. Mickey Mantle

B. Lou Gehrig

C. Ted Williams

D. Babe Ruth

A: ***D. Babe Ruth.*** Babe Ruth hit 714 home runs in his career which ended in 1935. For 38 years, Ruth, who was nicknamed Sultan of Swat because he hit so many home runs, held the record. In 1936, Babe Ruth became one of the first players elected to the Baseball Hall of Fame.

Hank Aaron almost broke Babe Ruth's home run record in 1973, but he ended the season with 713 career home runs. Aaron, nicknamed Hammerin' Hank because he could hit the ball hard, like a hammer striking a nail, set a record early the next season, when he hit his 715th career home run. Aaron, an African American, was criticized by many people when he was getting close to breaking Ruth's record. Some baseball fans did not like the idea of a black man breaking the record set by Ruth, commonly thought of as an American hero because of his great talent.

Although Aaron was under a tremendous amount of pressure because of hostile fans, death threats he had received, and the prospect of breaking the home run record, he was still able to focus on his job, playing good baseball and hitting home runs. Fortunately, no harm came to Aaron, who succeeded in hitting more home runs than any other major leaguer. He still holds one of baseball's most famous records. Aaron was elected to the Baseball Hall of Fame in 1982.

Trivia Teaser #7

"I was big when I was growing up. When I was in high school, people started pitching around me because they didn't want to pitch to me. [But] baseball wasn't my main sport. Football and basketball were my favorite sports. I had never taken baseball seriously before high school. I dreamed and I believed I was going to be in the big leagues and it happened." *I play for the Chicago White Sox. My nickname is the Big Hurt, and I like to hit home runs. I have something in common with four Baseball Hall of Famers—Jimmie Foxx, Babe Ruth, Ted Williams, and Lou Gehrig. WHO AM I?*

GRRR!

Who holds the major league record for most home runs in one season?

A. Roger Maris
B. Babe Ruth
C. Hank Aaron
D. Cecil Fielder

Roger Maris sends the ball out of the stadium.

A. Roger Maris. In 1961 Maris hit 61 home runs while playing for the New York Yankees. Only one other player has hit at least 60 home runs in a single major league season. Do you know who? Babe Ruth. Ruth hit 60 home runs in 1927. Ruth held the single-season home run record for 33 years, until Maris set his own mark in 1961. Ruth and Maris have something e!se in common. Both were playing for the New York Yankees when they reached 60 home runs.

In 1996 Mark McGwire of the Oakland Athletics (commonly known as the A's) was the only major league player with more than 50 home runs. He hit 52. In 1987 McGwire hit 49 homers. Ken Griffey Jr. of the Seattle Mariners hit 45 home runs in 1993, 40 in 1994, and 49 in 1996. The Texas Rangers' Juan Gonzalez has also hit more than 40 home runs in three different seasons—in 1996 (47), 1993 (46), and 1992 (43). Someday one of these players, or perhaps someone else, may be able to hit more than 61 home runs to break Roger Maris's record.

Trivia Teaser #8

What is a designated hitter
and who was baseball's first?

Chapter 3

Women and Baseball

Women have played baseball since the end of the Civil War. The earliest teams were organized at colleges for women. Women formed teams at Vassar College in upstate New York as early as 1866. Vassar's female baseball players and women players from other colleges were criticized because many people at that time did not think women should be allowed to play baseball. They thought that only men should play what they believed to be a rough sport.

In 1875 the first women's professional club was started in Springfield, Illinois. On September 11, 1875, a game was played between two of the club's teams—the Blondes and the Brunettes. This game is thought to have been the first contest featuring female professional baseball players. Women continued to play baseball through the nineteenth century and into the twentieth century.

A woman struck out two future Baseball Hall of Famers in a professional baseball game. True or False?

True. Jackie Mitchell was 17 years old when she became the first woman to sign a contract with a men's professional baseball team. In 1931, she signed with the Chattanooga Lookouts, a minor league team located in Tennessee. In early April 1931, Mitchell pitched for the Lookouts in an exhibition game against the New York Yankees. Mitchell's first batter was Babe Ruth. She struck him out on three straight pitches. The next batter was Lou Gehrig who was also struck out by the 17-year-old. Mitchell was taken out of the game after throwing two balls to the next batter.

Jackie Mitchell knew a lot about baseball before her game against the Yankees. She had been taught how to pitch by a former player named Dazzy Vance who, many

years later, would also be elected to Baseball's Hall of Fame. After Mitchell's game against the Yankees, her Lookouts' contract was canceled by major league baseball's commissioner who did not believe women should play professional baseball. She never pitched again for Chattanooga.

Jackie Mitchell

Did You Know?

During World War II, a professional baseball league for women was established. The All American Girls Professional Baseball League (AAGPBL) was created in 1942. The league, with teams in Illinois, Indiana, Wisconsin, Michigan, and Minnesota, stayed in business for 12 seasons, 1943–1954. Many of the best women ballplayers of those days played professional baseball in the AAGPBL, with the highest salaries reaching $125 per week. The All American Girls Professional Baseball League is commemorated in a permanent exhibit at the National Baseball Hall of Fame.

The AAGPBL made history on July 1, 1943. On that date, two teams from the All American Girls Professional Baseball League played in the first night baseball game ever held at Wrigley Field, a ballpark in Chicago, Illinois. The field did not have permanent lights, so temporary lighting was installed just for the AAGPBL ball game. The Chicago Cubs, a men's major league team, also played their games in Wrigley Field—as they still do. The Cubs did not play a night game at Wrigley Field until August 9, 1988, 45 years after women did it first.

Mickey Maguire whacks one for the Muskegon Lassies of the AAGPBL.

Trivia Teaser #9

What is the name of the 1992 movie that told the story of the All American Girls Professional Baseball League?

Did You Know?

In addition to female baseball players, several women umpires have worked in professional baseball, although none have participated in a regular-season major league baseball game. In the 1970s and 1980s, Pam Postema was a minor league baseball umpire. Although she never umpired a regular big league game, she did umpire several spring training games between major league teams. In 1989, she became the first woman to umpire in Class AAA, the highest level in professional baseball's minor leagues.

The Colorado Silver Bullets are a leading women's professional baseball team. They travel around the country, mainly playing against men's amateur teams. In 1996 Pamela Davis, one of the Silver Bullets, became the first woman to pitch for a men's pro team in more than 40 years. She pitched for the Jacksonville (Florida) Suns, a minor league baseball team, in a game against the Australian men's Olympic baseball team. Davis pitched for one inning, striking out one batter and giving up one hit and no runs.

In 1997 Ila Borders became the first woman to pitch in a regular season pro baseball game when she joined up with the Class A Northern League.

Did You Know?

Toni Stone was probably the first woman to play regularly for a men's professional baseball team during the season. In 1953 and 1954, she played second base for the Indianapolis Clowns and Kansas City Monarchs of the Negro leagues. People thought she was a strong, tough player who could play as hard as any male player. She even batted .243 in 1953, her first professional baseball season. Stone began playing baseball in high school. When she was 15 years old, she played on a men's softball team in her hometown of St. Paul, Minnesota. In 1993, Toni was elected to the Women's Sports Hall of Fame.

Chapter 4

Statistics

Baseball may have more statistics to keep track of than any other sport. There are also rules to follow for figuring out each statistic. Statistics are used to tell how players are doing and to compare them with other players. Earned run average (ERA) and batting average (BA) are baseball's most common statistics.

Roger Clemens of the Toronto Blue Jays lets go of a pitch during a game against the Oakland Athletics.

An ERA is the average number of earned runs, or runs scored without the assistance of fielding errors, given up by a pitcher in a full nine-inning game. To figure out a pitcher's ERA, multiply the number of earned runs given up by nine—the number of innings in a complete game—and then divide by the number of innings that pitcher has pitched.

If Roger Clemens pitches six innings and gives up two earned runs, his ERA can be figured this way:

$$2 \times 9 = 18$$
$$18 \div 6 = 3.00$$

Earned run averages are always carried out to two decimal points. If an ERA calculation results in a number with more than two digits after the decimal point, the number is rounded up or down, depending on whether the third digit after the decimal point is less than five (round down) or five or more (round up). ERAs under 3.00 are considered excellent.

$$2 \times 9 = 18$$
$$18 \div 6 = 3.00$$

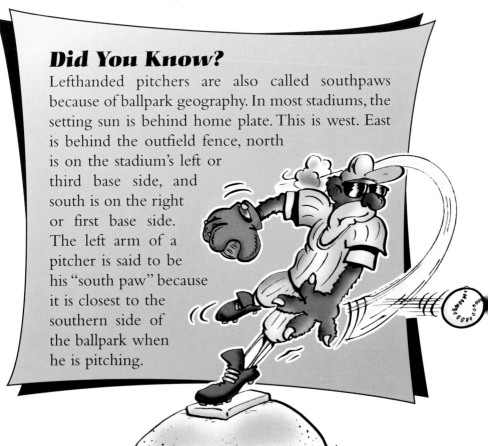

Did You Know?

Lefthanded pitchers are also called southpaws because of ballpark geography. In most stadiums, the setting sun is behind home plate. This is west. East is behind the outfield fence, north is on the stadium's left or third base side, and south is on the right or first base side. The left arm of a pitcher is said to be his "south paw" because it is closest to the southern side of the ballpark when he is pitching.

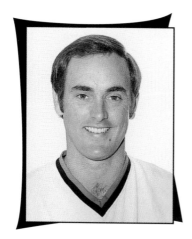

Nolan Ryan

Let's compare the ERAs of some of baseball's best pitchers. Nolan Ryan pitched for 27 years in the major leagues. He pitched 5,387 innings and gave up 1,911 earned runs. What was Nolan's ERA? Multiply 1,911 earned runs by nine.

$$\begin{array}{r} 1{,}911 \\ \times\ \ 9 \\ \hline 17{,}199 \end{array}$$

Then, divide 17,199 by 5,387 innings pitched. Nolan Ryan's career ERA is 3.192686. The third digit after the decimal point is less than five, so drop all the numbers after the nine to get Nolan's official ERA, 3.19.

Greg Maddux of the Atlanta Braves has an ERA of 2.87. In 11 major league seasons, he has pitched 2365.2 innings, giving up 753 earned runs. Multiply 753 earned runs by nine.

$$\begin{array}{r} 753 \\ \times\ 9 \\ \hline 6{,}777 \end{array}$$

OK, what's next? If you divided 6,777 by 2,365.2 innings pitched, you were right. That will give you Greg's career ERA of 2.87.

Did You Know?

The lowest career ERA in baseball history is 1.82. This was achieved by Ed Walsh, who pitched for 14 years, from 1904 to 1917. He is a member of Baseball's Hall of Fame.

Ed Walsh

Trivia Teaser #10

What if in one season the New York Yankees' Andy Pettitte pitched 150 innings and gave up 50 earned runs, while John Smoltz of the Atlanta Braves gave up 70 earned runs in 200 innings. Who would have the lowest ERA?

A batting average is the number of hits a batter records divided by the batter's appearances at the plate. Like ERAs, batting averages are expressed in decimal places. But unlike earned run averages, BA numbers are fractions, and all digits are to the right of the decimal point, like .325, .276, .289.

To figure out a batting average, divide a player's hits into his official at bats (the times when a batter comes to the plate, not including when he walks, hits a sacrifice, or is hit by a pitch). If Cal Ripken Jr. has 10 official at-bats and three hits, his batting average can be figured this way:

$$3 \div 10 = .300$$

Batting averages over .300 are considered to be excellent.

Trivia Teaser #11

"From day one, I always wanted to be a baseball player. I always worked real hard in every sport but baseball was the sport to be for me. Cal Ripken Jr. has been my role model for a long time." *Like Cal, I am a shortstop for a major league team. I play for the Seattle Mariners. WHO AM I?*

Q: *Let's compare batting averages for some of baseball's best players. In the 1996 season, Mo Vaughn of the Boston Red Sox had 207 hits in 635 at bats. The Oakland A's Mark McGwire recorded 132 hits in 423 at bats. What are their batting averages?*

A: *Mark McGwire's 1996 batting average was .3120. Mo Vaughn's was .3259.* Because the third digit in McGwire's figure is zero, drop it. The third digit in Vaughn's, a nine, rounds the figure up to .326.

Did You Know?

Ty Cobb has the highest career batting average in baseball history. His average is .367.

Ty Cobb

Trivia Teaser #12

Let's say Cal Ripken Jr. comes to bat 500 times in one season and he gets 140 hits. What is his batting average?

Chapter 5

Baseball's Best Players

Since major league baseball began more than 100 years ago, there have been many great players. Most of their records and statistics have been recorded. Knowing batting averages and earned run averages helps baseball fans to compare players and find out who is the best.

Here is a list of some of the greatest players in baseball history, based on statistics. In the six different categories, the top five players are listed—those with the most hits, the most home runs, the highest batting averages, the lowest earned run averages, the most wins, and the most strikeouts. Some of the best players of the 1990s are also included. You can see how their career statistics compare to the best in baseball history.

Pete Rose

Hank Aaron

BATTING

Most Hits

Pete Rose	4,256
Ty Cobb	4,191
Hank Aaron	3,771
Stan Musial	3,630
Tris Speaker	3,514

Current Players

Tony Gwynn	2,780
Cal Ripken Jr.	2,715
Barry Larkin	1,547
Kenny Lofton	1,047
Mike Piazza	875

Most Home runs

Hank Aaron	755
Babe Ruth	714
Willie Mays	660
Frank Robinson	586
Harmon Killebrew	573

Fred McGriff	339
Cecil Fielder	302
Matt Williams	279
Ken Griffey Jr.	294
Frank Thomas	257

Highest Batting Average

Ty Cobb	.367
Rogers Hornsby	.358
Joe Jackson	.356
Ed Delahanty	.346
Tris Speaker	.345

Current Players

Tony Gwynn	.340
Ken Griffey Jr.	.302
Barry Larkin	.299
Barry Bonds	.288
Cal Ripken Jr.	.276

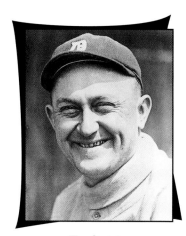

Ty Cobb

Cy Young

Ed Walsh

PITCHING

Most Wins

Cy Young	511
Walter Johnson	416
Christy Matthewson	373
Grover C. Alexander	373
Warren Spahn	363

Current Players

Roger Clemens	213
Greg Maddux	184
John Smoltz	129
Randy Johnson	124
Mike Mussina	105

Lowest ERA

Ed Walsh	1.82
Addie Joss	1.88
Three Finger Brown	2.06
Monte Ward	2.10
Christy Matthewson	2.13

Greg Maddux	2.81
Orel Hershiser	3.25
David Cone	3.13
Tom Glavine	3.40
Kevin Brown	3.42

Most Strikeouts

Nolan Ryan	5,714
Steve Carlton	4,136
Bert Blyleven	3,701
Tom Seaver	3,640
Don Sutton	3,574

Current Players

Randy Johnson	2,000
Greg Maddux	1,820
Orel Hershiser	1,786
Jack McDowell	1,254
Hideo Nomo	703

Nolan Ryan

Trivia Teaser Answers

#1 *Answer: Catchers and first basemen do not wear gloves.* They wear mitts, short for the word mittens. Like mittens, mitts do not have spaces for each individual finger. Catchers and first basemen catch the most thrown balls during a baseball game, and these balls are usually thrown very hard. Mitts have more padding and shielding for the fingers than gloves do, protecting these players' hands from being injured or broken by a thrown baseball.

Catcher's mitt

First baseman's mitt

#2 *Answer: Bullpens are where relief pitchers warm up before entering a game.* At the ballpark, each team has its own bullpen. They are located either down the right and left field foul lines or behind the outfield fence. In the early twentieth century, the professional baseball team in Durham, North Carolina, played in a ballpark that had a large wooden sign with a picture of a bull painted on it. Games were played during the day. To stay cool in the summer, pitchers who were not playing used to sit in the shade under the sign behind the outfield fence. Soon, people began to say the pitchers were down in the "bull pen." Use of this word quickly spread, and the term is still used to describe the place where relief pitchers watch the game and throw practice pitches. So, although real bulls never lived in baseball bullpens, a bull made of wood once did!

#3 *Answer: Nine.* In baseball's earliest days, a game was played until a team scored 21 or more points. In 1857, the nine-inning game was established. Overtime innings are played, however, if the score is tied after nine innings of play.

#4 *Answer: Brooklyn Dodgers.* The Dodgers played in Brooklyn, one of the five boroughs that make up New York City, from 1897 until 1957, the year after Jackie Robinson's career ended. In 1957 the Dodgers moved to Los Angeles, California, where they still play.

#5 *Answer: Rickey Henderson.* In 1982 Henderson played for the Oakland A's and stole 130 bases. This beat the existing record of 118 set by Lou Brock in 1974, when he played for the St. Louis Cardinals. Lou Brock is a member of the Baseball Hall of Fame.

Rickey Henderson

#6

Answer: Cecil Fielder. Fielder and Babe Ruth are the only players ever to lead the major leagues in runs batted in (RBIs) three years in a row. Fielder did it in 1990, 1991, and 1992. Babe did it in 1919, 1920, and 1921. From 1990 to 1996, Fielder blasted 257 home runs—more than any other major league hitter.

Cecil Fielder   Frank Thomas

#7

Answer: Frank Thomas. In 1993 Thomas became the fifth player in major league history to bat over .300, with 20 or more home runs, and 100 or more walks, runs, and runs batted in for each of three straight years. Babe Ruth (1919, 1920, 1921), Lou Gehrig (1929, 1930, 1931, 1932 and 1934, 1935, 1936, 1937), Ted Williams (1946, 1947, 1948, 1949) and Jimmie Foxx (1934, 1935, 1936) are the only other players to accomplish this feat, and they are all members of the Baseball Hall of Fame. In 1996 Frank Thomas became the only player ever to record these statistics for six straight years.

#8

Answer: American League games all begin with 10 players on the game roster for each team. The 10th player is called the designated hitter (DH). This player does not play in the field but is "designated," or picked by the manager, to be only a hitter in the game. When a designated hitter is used, the team's pitcher does not come up to bat. Instead, the pitcher's only job is to pitch. *Ron Blomberg of the New York Yankees became the first designated hitter in 1973, the first year teams in the American League could use the DH.* The designated hitter is not used in the National League.

Answer: **A League of their Own,** starring Geena Davis, Tom Hanks, and Madonna.

Answer: Let's see: multiply Andy Pettitte's 50 earned runs by nine.

$$50 \times 9 = 450$$
$$450 \div 150 = 3.00$$

Next, John Smoltz. 70 earned runs multiplied by nine.

$$70 \times 9 = 630$$
$$630 \div 200 = 3.15$$

Andy Pettitte's ERA of 3.00 is lower.

#11 *Answer: Alex Rodriguez.* The 1996 season was Rodriguez's first full season in the major leagues. Only 21 years old, he batted .358, hitting 36 home runs and batting in 123 runs.

Alex Rodriguez   Cal Ripken Jr.

#12 *Answer: Ripken's batting average is .280.* Divide Ripken's hits by his at bats.

$$140 \div 500 = .280$$

#13 *Answer: Pitchers don't use their knuckles to throw knuckleballs.* They hold the ball tightly, with their fingertips or fingernails touching one of the ball's seams. Instead of having their fingers flat on the ball, their fingers and knuckles look like they are standing up on top of the baseball. Knuckleballs are thought to be one of the hardest pitches to hit, because they confuse batters by the way they move and jump on their way to home plate.

Resources to Check Out

Books

Dickson, Paul. *The Dickson Baseball Dictionary*. New York: Facts on File, 1989.

Galt, Margot Fortunato. *Up to the Plate: The All American Girls Professional Baseball League*. Minneapolis: Lerner Publications Company, 1995.

Geng, Don. *Fundamental Baseball*. Minneapolis: Lerner Publications Company, 1995.

Honig, Donald. *Baseball: The Illustrated History of America's Game*. New York: Crown Publishing Group, 1990.

Obojski, Robert. *Baseball's Strangest Moments*. New York: Sterling Publishing Co., Inc., 1988.

Tygiel, Jules. *Baseball's Great Experiment: Jackie Robinson and his Legacy*. New York: Oxford University Press, Inc., 1983.

Web sites

Major League Baseball homepage:
http://www.majorleaguebaseball.com

All American Girls Professional Baseball League homepage:
http://www.dlcwest.com/~smudge/index.html

Negro leagues historical archives:
http://www.fastball.com/hotlist.htm

National Baseball Hall of Fame and Museum homepage:
http://www.enews.com/bas_hall_fame/overview.com

Bibliography

Adelson, Bruce, et. al. *The Minor League Baseball Book.* Old Tappan, NJ: Macmillan, 1995.

Dickson, Paul. *The Dickson Baseball Dictionary.* New York: Facts on File, 1989.

Riley, James A. *The Baseball Encyclopedia of the Negro Baseball Leagues.* New York: Carroll & Graf Publishers, 1994.

Thorn, John and Pete Palmer, eds. *Total Baseball.* New York: Warner Books, 1989.

Baseball Encyclopedia: The Complete and Definitive Record of Major League Baseball. Ninth edition. New York: Macmillan, 1993.

The Sporting News Baseball Register. St. Louis, MO: The Sporting News Publishing Co., 1996.

About the Author

Bruce Adelson is a sports writer, substitute teacher, and former attorney whose published works include *The Minor League Baseball Book*. His work has also appeared in The Four Sport Stadium Guide and in publications such as *The Washington Post, Sport Magazine,* and *Baseball America.* The Sports Trivia books are his first children's publications. Adelson lives in Arlington, Virginia.

About the Illustrator

Harry Pulver Jr. is an illustrator and animator who also plays the accordian and guitar. His work has appeared in numerous national ad campaigns and in books, including *Find It!* and *Tracking the Facts,* two other titles by Lerner Publications.